Spirit Guides

Spirit Guides for Beginners

The Complete Guide to Contacting Your
Spirit Guide and Communicating
with the Spirit World

Mia Rose

LIMIT OF LIABILITY/DISCLAIMER OF WARRANTY:

All rights reserved. No part of this book may be reproduced or transmitted in any form or by any means, electronic, mechanical, magnetic, photographic including photocopying, recording or by any information storage and retrieval system, without prior written permission of the publisher. The publisher and the author make no representations or warranties with respect to the accuracy or completeness of the contents of this work and specifically disclaim all warranties of fitness for a particular purpose. This work is sold with the understanding that the author and the publisher are not engaged in rendering legal, advice-based, or other professional services. If professional assistance is required, the services of a competent professional person should be sought. Although every precaution has been taken in the preparation of this book, neither the publisher nor the author shall be liable for damages arising herefrom.

copyright © 2014 by Mia Rose, all rights reserved.

Introduction

I want to thank you for giving me the opportunity to spend some time with you.

For the last 10 years of my life I have studied, practiced, and shared my love of spirituality and internal development. I kept diaries for years documenting the incredible changes that graced my life. This passion for writing has blossomed into a new chapter in my life where publishing books has become a full-time career.

I feel extremely blessed and fortunate to have the opportunity to share my message with you. Each of my books are written to inspire others to explore the many aspects of their internal world. My goal is to touch the lives of others in a positive way and be a catalyst for positive change in this world.

I am forever grateful for your support and I know you will get immense value through my books. I am really looking forward to serving you and giving you great insight into my passions.

Your friend,

Mia Rose

Table of Contents

Chapter 1 When Shamans and Science Agree 1

Chapter 2 First Steps and Safety Steps for Meeting Your Guides 5

Chapter 3 Cleopatra of Egypt, Mary of Bethlehem, or Maureen from the launderette? 11

Chapter 4 *Is* There Anybody There? 17

Chapter 5 Dealing with Unwelcome Presences (and Twitter) 23

Chapter 6 First Steps to Spiritual Communication . 27

Chapter 7 The Ways of the Spirit World 33

Chapter 8 Who Exactly Are You Dealing With? 39

Chapter 9 Building Spiritual Relationships 43

Conclusion 51

Other books by Mia Rose 53

Chapter 1
When Shamans and Science Agree

Many millennia have passed since we took our first tentative steps down from the trees, shakily walked upright for the first time and began to develop the earliest civilizations. Since then we've come on in leaps and bounds. We've conquered the world. We've even conquered space! Yet amongst all that civilization we have seemingly lost an important part of ourselves. Back in those pre-human days, we were simply another species of mammal. Our early, ancient ancestors instinctively understood not only this simple fact but saw the connections between ourselves and all living creatures -- from trees to birds to wild animals!

Many of these ancient cultures also had strong traditions which recognize the world of "spirit" beyond the visible world. This world is a deeper expression of an understanding of the interconnectivity of all things. For our study, it is beneficial to examine some of these cultures and beliefs. For example, Shamanic traditions can be found in all cultures and appear to have their roots back before the dawn of time. It is widely believed to be the most ancient form of religious expression, reaching back into the paleolithic era.

Shamans communicate with spirits – be that human, animal, or non-living entities - in order to mediate between the manifested world and the spirit world. Their roles are varied but a strong focus on healing can be found in most shamanic traditions. These traditions also focus on the connected nature of all life (not just human) and as such they have long since preempted modern science in understanding how our actions have implications and consequences that affect the wider world.

It's not really rocket science to understand that by using up the world's resources we will all be poorer, and that by destroying both habitat and many species we may well be upsetting the finely tuned balance that makes our world inhabitable. Science has caught up, although it's taken some time, on these facts and now modern scientists often acknowledge that many of the teachings of ancient cultures and shamanic traditions are not myth and fantasy but instead have solid groundings in fact. So, why do so many seem to neglect this enlightening aspect of life?

The world of spirit can be difficult or even worrisome for people to understand and to come to terms with. It may seem to conflict with the individual's religious or personal beliefs. Or you may be thinking that there isn't any scientific evidence for a spirit world. But there is! Even modern science can offer some understanding of how the universe itself operates on a deeper level. Current science understands that we are all nothing more than a collection of atoms and energy. None of the atoms or the energy that is "us" suddenly comes into existence when we are born, nor does it absolutely disappear when we die. In fact, the collection of material and energy that is "us" is simply a temporary, random formation, which creates a living, breathing human being. When we die this energy continues to exist in different forms, just as it existed before we lived. Much like many other aspects of science, we cannot see this energy without the proper "tools". Consider all that we've discovered in the universe and how much of it we wouldn't be able to even know it existed without modern technology.

In many shamanic and spiritualist traditions, this energy, the spirit, is recognized. We are merely a vibration within the universe which can manifest in different forms – before, during, and after our life on earth. Many traditions believe that the human soul is in a cycle of learning and evolution, that we exist in both the spirit and visible realms, and that we may experience many reincarnations gradually learning, evolving, and developing a higher wisdom. Of course, many of us have often wondered why we're here. And that begs to question, how are we to achieve this seemingly unknown purpose?

This process can take many reincarnations and some more highly evolved souls choose to remain in spirit form to guide those of us here on earth. Ultimately, we all will transform into a purer form, but for many of us we must learn many lessons before this transition is made. In some religious traditions, spirit guides are expressed as enlightened souls such as the Buddha or Saints and Prophets. Although their physical form is gone from the earth, their spirit remains present in the spirit world and can offer guidance and assistance to those still living on earth.

In shamanic traditions, it is the shaman who mediates and communicates with this wider world of spirit, interceding on behalf of either individuals or whole communities to access the aid of spirits. However, we all have spirit guides – whether we realize it or not – and learning to work with these guides and communicate with them is possible for anybody. You don't have to be an experienced shaman or psychic to begin your spiritual journey.

In this book we'll look at how to begin that process, what spirit guides are in more detail, and how to work with them. We'll also take a look at some of the do's and don'ts of working with spirits, how to stay safe and how to ensure that you benefit from working with spirits.

Chapter 2
First Steps and Safety Steps for Meeting Your Guides

The spirit world is all around us. We are, in fact, part of it. Most people go through their lives with only a limited awareness, if any, of this wider existence. The occasional glimpse from the corner of your eye of somebody or something which isn't actually "there". Sudden, unexpected coincidences, which may be beneficial or otherwise. Sounds that may or may not be real, a door which opens unexpectedly and can't quite be explained away by the breeze. All of these are "signs" of the unseen, or half-seen, presence of the other planes of existence.

Certain people are born with an innate ability to sense the spirit world far more clearly than others. These people may come from a long line of clairvoyants, mediums, and psychics, while in some cases these skills seem to spring from nowhere. It is often highly evolved souls who possess these skills, and many of them will tell you that while working with the spirit world can be a great pleasure and blessing, at other times it can be onerous and very burdensome.

While some individuals are born with natural skills at working with the spirit world and spirit guides, it is possible for all of us to learn the techniques which are required to do so. Keep in mind that opening yourself up to this world has its dangers. Not all spirits necessarily have your best interests at heart. Some are kind and good, others mischievous and troublesome, while yet others have less healthy (or helpful) purposes in mind. Many spirits were once humans and, like humans, have their own agendas. Learning to protect yourself when communicating with this other world, and with the beings which inhabit it, is essential. We will cover some basic ways in which to protect yourself as you begin this journey in this chapter.

Even though some spirits may have a troubling agenda, your spirit guides are very much on your side and you have no need to fear them! These guides will be there to help you achieve your life's purposes. These goals are set out before we incarnate in the world of flesh. Many spiritualists believe that it is at this stage, before incarnation, that we choose our guides. It can be empowering to realize that well before we were born, a plan was in place and these premortal connections and relationships were established. Unfortunately, many of us are blind to our guides' existence once we become real in this world. Accessing their help and guidance is a slow step by step process, if you are not naturally attuned to the technique, and can take time to master. However, it is well worth it and once mastered, working with your spirit guides can help you to achieve your goals both in this world and the next.

Creating the Right Atmosphere

It's not completely impossible for those of us who have natural clairvoyant skills, but it's fairly unlikely that communing with the spirit world will be achieved in a room with the TV, radio, internet or a horde of young children. While experienced shamans and spiritualists can contact spirits in many and varied different settings, even they often retreat to places of silence where distraction is minimized as they take their first steps to working with the spirit world. Complete lack of distraction is required for those first learning these skills.

Shamans and spiritualists connect with the spirit world by entering an altered state. Many exciting techniques and substances have been used across the millennia, but these should generally be avoided for the novice. To lift the veil between the worlds safely, a deep state of meditation is required.

Tools of the Trade

You'll need some helpful tools before you begin, and these should be assembled before you start the process of contacting your spirit guides. You should assemble these before you cast a circle in which to work (see below) in order not to break that circle once it is cast. The "tools" you'll need are:

- A comfortable space to sit; you can choose to sit on the floor on cushions, but a chair is perfectly acceptable.

- Loose fitting, comfortable clothes, appropriate to your setting (indoors or outdoors). Comfort is key here. Make sure you won't become too hot or too cold and choose your clothing according to your location.

- A blanket is often useful to have on hand. Meditating will relax you, slow your heart rate and can reduce your circulation, meaning you may feel cold during a longer session.

- Pen, paper and/or notebook.

- Spiritual or religious symbols which you feel are appropriate (this is optional). Symbols can help us to focus our thoughts, but they can also be distracting, so try with or without to see what works for you.

- A candle. This is useful for focus and the light is also believed to attract the attention of the spirits. Scented or otherwise is up to you, though scented may be distracting.

- Incense. Sandalwood is a good choice, as it offers protection and clarity. Again, the scent can be distracting initially but sandalwood is generally recommended as being helpful, so try simply burning it around the house for a few days until you've become used to the smell.

Casting a Circle

This is a traditional technique used in many spiritual settings and is often seen as casting a "spell". Don't be put off by the word spell! This is merely a part of ritual, and rituals can be found in every spiritual and religious tradition around the world. In terms of working with the spirits the aim is to create a safe, defined space. In many other traditions a similar process takes place before a ritual begins. This can include building whole churches or temples to create a sacred space or simply conducting blessings with Holy Water and incense before praying. Casting a circle is no different; it is about purifying a place, creating a sacred space and fortifying the sense of protection.

In this case, "casting a circle" simply means creating a safe, ritual, sacred space. There are no strict rules as to the words used in this ritual – express the sentiments outlined below in a way in which you feel comfortable.

- Identify the four points of the compass, north, south, east and west.

- Facing north, bow and say, "I cast this circle with light and love to protect myself from unwanted, harmful spirits".

- Turning clockwise, repeat this statement to the east, then (turning clockwise again) to the south, then the west and finally turn to the north again.

- Now, turning slowly pointing at the "outline" of the circle, turn three times, clockwise through the points of the compass, visualizing light illuminating the boundary.

With the circle cast you should now be able to begin working safely with the spirit world and your spirit guides. When you have finished your session, don't forget to open the circle. The protective circle is created using spirit and earth energy and leaving it in place needlessly wastes this energy. To open the circle simply face north and thank the spirits and the earth for providing the energy of protection, turn anti-clockwise this time and repeat the process to the west, south and east (repeating the process three times). As you do so, imagine the light at the boundary of the circle gently fading away.

Chapter 3
Cleopatra of Egypt, Mary of Bethlehem, or Maureen from the launderette?

Everything has a spirit, and spirit guides come in various shapes and sizes. Don't expect Elvis or the Virgin Mary to turn up and, likewise, don't expect Nero or Cleopatra. Many people *do* hope that great figures from history will be their spirit guides, and many people are disappointed when they are not. Spirit guides are who and what they are, not who and what we expect them to be. In fact, we may have chosen them before we incarnate, and our higher selves will have chosen the right people for us. Hold tight to truth and know that your guides, whoever they may be, are exactly who you need.

In some cases, spirit guides will be with us for life and in others they will only appear in our existence for a period (long or short). In general, spirit guides are the souls of people not currently incarnated in human form, and many wish purely to help us. This means that rather than Cleopatra, you may discover a guide who was once a chimney sweep in nineteenth century London, or a laundry woman from sixteenth century Marseilles. Spirit guides really do come in all shapes and sizes – and some of them may be a surprise!

There are different types of spirit guides and these are discussed in more detail in throughout this chapter.

Ascended Masters

These spirit guides are usually people who have led many reincarnated existences here on earth, gradually evolving to a higher level of consciousness and a state of enlightenment. Their journey in this world is over and they are ready to move on to higher planes of existence. However, before continuing their own journey many choose to selflessly remain in spirit form to aid those of us in the physical world to learn, develop and attain greater states of enlightenment. We all, including the spirits of Ascended Masters, are on the same journey; these spirits have simply chosen to aid us all in that path. Buddha, Krishna, and Christ have all been identified as souls who have achieved this higher state.

These may be the "celebrities" of the spirit world but there are many, many more of this type of soul, both male and female. These spirit guides will normally not work with just one soul, and their focus being on helping humanity as a whole. You may find that you are one of many people that these souls are working with and aiding, and they can offer a high level of insight into your own life and your place and purpose in the world. In the early stages of learning to work with spirit guides, it's not very likely that you will encounter these beings – although it's certainly not unheard of! The longer you practice the art of working within the spirit world, the more likely it is that you will come to meet and experience these celebrities of the spirit world.

Chapter 3

Meet the Ancestors

Ancestor worship and veneration is extremely common across many cultures and seems to have formed an intrinsic part of many ancient religious systems. It's something that even those of us who live in modern, western societies have never really shaken off! Many of us remember with love the relatives that we have lost, light candles for them (even if we are not terribly religious in other areas of life), and will often think of them when dealing with difficult issues in our lives.

Our ancestors form part of us, physically and emotionally, and have shaped who we are. It should be no great surprise to those working with spirit guides that this focus is a two-way thing. Recently deceased relatives often show a keen interest in those working in the spirit world and more distant relatives, who passed to the world of spirit centuries ago, often appear as spirit guides. In many cases it's the spirits of our ancestors, recent and ancient, who we encounter when we first explore the world of the spirit. These spirits are, largely, the most protective, helpful, and able to offer the best guidance and advice. It is, after all, in their interests to keep us safe and see us prosper!

The Archetype

This type of spirit guide will appear in a guise that should be easily recognizable. A healer, a warrior, a storyteller, a lover or a priest/ess. These guides appear at certain times in our lives to help us with a specific path that we must travel, obstacles that we must negotiate or lessons that we need to learn. Many saints in different religious traditions incorporate specific, archetypal qualities and are used, within those traditions, to teach specific lessons, to intercede on our behalf in those areas or to simply be a focus for understanding certain areas of life. Archetypes are very much like "patron saints"; they guide us with a great depth of insight, knowledge, and power in what are often difficult and dark times. If you encounter an Archetype, it's vital to take note of their messages or guidance; these spirit guides appear only when we have an urgent need of their guidance and should not be ignored.

Animal Guides

The world of spirit is less complicated (and more complicated) than the visible world. Relationships between human and the non-human are interwoven. This is, of course, true in the physical world but is expressed more obviously in the spirit world. In Native American traditions this has been long recognized, and animals are used as totems, forming a significant part of the shamanic tradition within their cultures. Throughout history humans have identified with the different traits of animals and these have been used to symbolize whole communities and countries (the Russian Bear, the American Eagle). In the world of spirit, however, the relationship between human and other living beings is much deeper and more complex. Many people will discover that their main spirit guide is an animal, or even the spirit of a tree! Our most ancient ancestors lived alongside the "real" versions of these spirits. Indeed, we were simply one species amongst many. In the spirit world this relationship continues, and animal spirit guides help to teach us important lessons in life. Unlike other spirit guides, often the focus here is "teaching" rather than guiding. Many animal spirit guides also provide companionship and protection in both the spirit world and the manifested world. Treat them with respect, love, and affection. They can be amongst the most companionable and protective of spirits, and many people experience the most fulfilling and enlightening relationships with these apparently humble spirits.

Taking the Leap

Hopefully, now you'll have an understanding of how to prepare to meet your spirit guides and what to expect from them. In the next chapter, we will look at contacting your spirit guides directly. The process can be slow and requires some patience, but with practice it will become second nature.

Chapter 4
Is There Anybody There?

You've cast a circle, you've meditated for hours and yet nothing! No spectral apparition has appeared in the living room and it's time to pack up and start preparing the evening meal. You've failed miserably at contacting your spirit guide. Or have you?

Spirit guides are not in the habit of giving command performances. Their presence is likely to be fairly constant, but it can take time to attune yourself to their presence. If your early efforts don't appear to be having any clear affect, don't be disenchanted. In fact, spirit guides will often work according to their own schedule. However, creating a space, time, and the right atmosphere in which to begin to sense their presence will encourage them to make themselves more apparent. Remember, they have always been with you even if you may not have been fully aware of them. The process is a little like tuning a TV set, or radio, except that you are the receiver and the transmissions are more delicate.

Meditation is the key to getting that fine-tuning process right. Learning meditation techniques can take time, and the most useful technique for contacting spirit guides can be mindfulness meditation. It focuses you clearly in the moment, on that candle burning in front of you, and at the same time creates a deep sense of relaxation and openness. This is the signal to your guides that you are ready to contact them. They may take their time, but they will take note of your readiness.

When you have established your circle, as described in Chapter 2, light your candle. Many people choose colored candles to represent a specific issue that they wish to find guidance on, but in the early days simply use a plain, white candle. Focus on the light, the flame of the candle and repeat over to yourself, "I wish to contact my spirit guide". Keep this thought in your head, repeating it over and over again. Simple steps and methods to keep in mind are:

- Don't have any preconceived notions of who (or what) your spirit guide is likely to be.

- Remain positive and avoid discussing what you are doing with skeptics – the negative energy of this can make the process more difficult to achieve with any success.

- Believe that you will make contact, but don't put a timescale on it.

Journals

Keeping a journal is a good way in which to record your progress and any contact you make with your spirit guide. Most of us have more than one spirit guide, usually from the different categories described in Chapter 3. In your early days of learning to work with spirit guides it's highly likely that you'll first encounter both ancestral spirits (though you may not recognize them) or animal spirit guides. In both cases, inquisitiveness is part of their reason for appearing. Be ready to welcome the presence of any guide who makes themselves known to you, and also to thank them, as you would any helpful visitor.

Spirits don't always appear fully formed and coherent in your life. A strong clue that you have made contact, without fully realizing it, is seeing a specific animal regularly. This may be a clue that an animal guide is in your life and has recognized your efforts to contact it. Seeing a stranger who reminds you of a relative or friend who has passed on, perhaps seeing them several times or so frequently that coincidence cannot explain the sighting, is also a strong sign that this spirit is making their presence felt. Sometimes smells, or sounds, or any number of other physical stimulus can suddenly bring back a memory of a person, or a feeling of them. Keep a note of these encounters and incidents in your life. This should give you plenty of evidence as to who or what is trying to make contact with you. Once you've decided, or established, who the spirit guide is, then focus your energy on them during your meditations.

Patience, the Ultimate Virtue

This process can take days, weeks, months or even longer, although the latter is extremely rare. However, at some point your spirit guide will appear more fully. You may see or hear them, or merely sense their presence at first. It's always nice to introduce yourself when you meet new people regardless of which plane of existence they exist on! Your spirit guide will, of course, already know you but it's wise to kindly introduce yourself at this point. If you recognize them (as in the case of a friend or relative who has passed on), tell them how pleased you are to see them. If not, simply introduce yourself and ask for their name. Wait for this to come to you; it will be provided, if not immediately. If the name is unfamiliar and/or unusual, then remember to write this down in your journal.

Message Waiting?

The next question to ask is whether they have anything they wish to tell you at this point. In many, many cases, they won't! This first encounter is simply that, a meeting. However, on occasion, important advice or information will be given at this stage. Don't forget to write this down and to take heed. Advice or information given during your first encounter is likely to be very significant and may be crucial for you. Don't forget to thank the spirit guide for any information that is given to you during the first (and subsequent) meetings and meditations.

Let's Get Physical

You'll know when you (or the guide) are ready to return to your own separate sphere of existence. Thank them again and tell them how important the meeting has been to you. Gradually allow yourself to rise gently and slowly back to consciousness. When you have tidied away the meditation tools and opened the circle it's wise to have a hot drink and something to eat. Working with the spirit world is simple and, if the advice in this book is followed, it's safe! However, you need to remember that you are living in the real, physical world, and simply eating and drinking are good ways to reestablish your connection to that world. The boundaries between the physical world and the spirit world need to be clearly defined in your life and breaking this link, once your session is over, is extremely important. Simple physical acts help to achieve this.

I See Dead People

Seeing dead people isn't normal, nor is it always a comfortable experience. While many people who communicate with spirits will find that they experience only a strong visualization, or sense of a presence, some of us do get a more detailed view. In fact, those who are most sensitive will experience a real, physical presence of their spirit guides. You may also come to the realization that you've always done this; dead people don't look so different to the rest of us and they can be hard to single out in a crowd.

This can be an unsettling experience, and if it's a very new experience it's worth seeking some advice and teaching from more experienced psychics, clairvoyants and/or spiritualists. Culturally, we also have often been trained to be "afraid" of death, or those who have passed over. There is very little sense to this. We're all going to make that natural transition and, in fact, have probably made it many times. The spirit world is only a continuation of this world and there is little to be afraid of.

Also, despite what Hollywood may wish us to believe, most of those who live in the spirit world don't display terrible disfigurements or have any strong desire to return to the physical world in a physical form. Headless horsemen/women are not as ubiquitous as you might have been led to believe and, in fact, most spirits will present a very happy, calm appearance. Most! In death, as in life, there's always one. Dealing with those more troublesome spirits is something that you will almost certainly encounter at some stage in your journey. Dealing with them and the consequences is what we'll be looking at in the next chapter.

Chapter 5
Dealing with Unwelcome Presences (and Twitter)

In life we can encounter some truly difficult characters, and in our dealings with the spirit world this is just as true as anywhere else. Communicating with the spirit world can generate some unwanted interest from spirits other than your own guides. It's a bit like Twitter, and as with Twitter, it's essential to keep a calm head when you do find unwanted "guests" in your presence. Your first line of defense is simple, practical good housekeeping! Creating a circle, or using other magical techniques like "smudging", or using prayer, are all good habits that you should employ before attempting to contact those in the spirit world.

Curiosity Killed the Cat but Didn't Stop it Being Curious

Unwanted spirits can come in different forms and even with good housekeeping, the odd one may slip through from time to time. There may be no intrinsically malevolent purpose to their presence, and they may simply have arrived through curiosity (this is the case surprisingly often). The spirit may even be one that has arrived to deliver a message but then decides it doesn't want to leave (again, annoyingly frequent). Remember, many spirits were once human, and they sometimes like the experience of being present in the physical world again so much that they wish to stay for a while. Can you blame them?

Missed Messages

Before you attempt to remove the unwanted spirit, be sure that it doesn't have an important message for you. It may be that it is not one of your regular guides, or that it needs to tell somebody in the physical world some important information. The spirit may even have got the wrong house! In this sense it may be trying to contact someone who is not in communication with the spirit world with an important message. Be sure before you tell the spirit to leave that it has had a chance to pass on whatever message it needs to and then thank it, asking it to leave.

Missing the Obvious

The simplest way to deal with an unwanted, uninvited, or over-staying spirit is an obvious one, and it's so obvious that many people fail to see it in the first place. Going back to the Twitter analogy, it's simply to block them! In the case of a spirit this can be done by telling them that you don't want them here. You need to be firm about this, so be blunt and don't be afraid to say it like you mean it. The words you choose can be whatever you feel is appropriate, but something as simple as "You are not welcome here, this is not the place for you" should in, most cases, be enough to deal with the problem. You can offer a blessing too, to soften the blow, and even thank them for their interest in you. Think of it as responding to a cold caller but be slightly less rude when slamming the receiver down.

Simply stating the fact that the spirit is not welcome is surprisingly effective in most cases. However, from time to time you'll find that a spirit is either stubborn, difficult, or even hostile. A cleansing spell, or blessing, are strongly recommended in this case. In the instance of a particularly difficult or hostile spirit, many of those who regularly work within the spirit world recommend working with a group of like-minded individuals to dislodge your unwanted guest. This is advisable in the more extreme cases and can make sense in even only mildly irritating cases if you are new to working with the spirit world.

Smudging

This is an easy, effective, and traditional 'cleansing' technique used for sacred spaces. It involves simply moving around the space with burning incense to purify the space and remove unwanted spirits. Most people will chant, possibly drumming in a rhythmic manner, speaking a spell or prayer to banish the unwanted presence. Circle the space clockwise, several times (three, six or nine are suggested) as you progress. An incense that is often used is sage, which has powerful associations with cleansing and banishing. Making your own smudging stick from homegrown, dried herbs is ideal for this purpose. The act of creating your own smudging stick reinforces your control, involvement and authority in the process and it often just feels "right". Your chanting should be appropriate to your purpose, so simply repeating the words or phrase "Spirit begone, you have no place here" will be enough to have a powerful affect. Don't assume you need complicated spells, incantations, robes, and wands. These are props and nothing more. Your intention is what counts (this is true in all areas of life), and firmly stating your intention can be done in whatever way you feel appropriate.

Don't be Afraid

Working with the spirit world can be startling, a little scary at first, and disorientating. Don't be afraid or let it scare you away from the spiritual growth that awaits you! It's an ancient practice and, importantly, the majority of spirits have no dark intentions. Your own spirit guides will be watching over you and protecting you. It's their presence and your own strength that will be important in your journey. Always be firm with the more difficult spirits and you will stay in control.

Chapter 6
First Steps to Spiritual Communication

If you have not previously practiced meditation or attempted to contact the spirit world, practice makes perfect. We've already taken a basic look at casting a circle, meditating, and inviting your spirit guides to make contact. It's possible, but unlikely that this will happen on the first attempt and you may need to practice for some time before you encounter your own personal guides. In fact, to make real, lasting contact with your spirit guides you will need to meditate daily to establish an initial connection and then, subsequently, a firm bond. In this chapter we'll look more closely at a detailed approach to contacting (and staying in contact with) your own guides.

The Basics of Belief

Remember, as you begin your journey that *everybody* has the ability and the potential to contact and work with the spirit world and spirit guides. There is no magical trick or knowledge that you require, and no special talent. We are all innately able to work with spirit guides, but the modern world does not focus on the spiritual side of life and many of us have repressed our natural abilities in this area, or simply discounted them. Belief is a crucial part of working with your spirit guides, and this is your first tool. Be open to your experiences and be prepared to take the process slowly. Although we all have the ability, if we have repressed, ignored, or dismissed these skills in the past it can take time to re-establish a connection with the spirit world and the spiritual side of ourselves. Be open, receptive, and willing to give time and gentle effort to the process. Think back to the analogy of finely tuning yourself: as the signals you receive become clearer you will also find that your belief in your own abilities grows. Here are some tips for successfully contacting your spirit guides:

- Begin the process by dimming the lights, closing the blinds, and lighting candles and/or incense as required. Not everyone finds incense helpful, as the fewer distractions for your senses in the physical world the better. This is a personal choice and it can be very much a case of trial and error.

- Many of those who regularly seek the advice of spirit guides recommend that apart from loose fitting, comfortable clothing you should avoid wearing much jewelry, and many prefer to work barefoot. Simplicity and lack of distraction are the key approaches to this kind of work.

- Choosing the right company both in this world and the other is not a bad idea. Some people choose to work with other mediums, especially early in their journey, while others feel more comfortable working alone. Spirit guides are often, if not nearly always, very personal to you and working alone is recommended in most cases.

- It's also equally important to consider the type of spirit you wish to attract. Remember that tuning-in process? In the early days, your calls may not be clear and, additionally, your clarity of vision may be 'fuzzy'. It's important, given these factors, to be clear about the types of spirit you wish to attract. There are many different types of entity in the spirit world and not all are beneficial. When beginning your meditation consider using a phrase like "I invite all of my own, loving and wise spirit guides to join me now, to come in peace and friendship". Remember that you can always chose the phrases and words that you are comfortable with and that are natural for you.

- Once you have created your circle and are comfortably sat within it breathe deeply, relax, and stretch. Continue to breathe in and out, focusing simply on this action and stretch until your body feels lighter, tension is lowered, and you begin to feel a sense of peace.

- Rhythmic drumming, or chanting, are often used to create the right atmosphere to encourage the presence of spirits. Chanting is the most practical alternative of the two, especially if you don't want the neighbors or other members of your household interrupting the process! The phrase "Om" repeated over and over will gradually help to induce the right frame of mind, clear from other thoughts, and reduce a close connection with the physical world around you.

- As your mind stills, you will begin to sense your "light body". This is the spiritual body with which we all are endowed when we incarnate in the world. It is this part of us that connects us to the spirit world, and this light body with which we enter its realm.

- You should pay close attention to the images that you will experience during this meditation. At first these images may not be clear but, with practice, they will become more real and physical. Most mediums describe the experience at this point as passing through a door. This is the gateway between the physical world and the spirit. It may, or may not, appear as a "door". For some it is simply a color, an archway or a sky filled with bright stars. As you pass through this door, again repeat your invitation to the spirits that you wish to accompany you.

- It is at this point that you are likely to see, or feel the presence of, your spirit guides. Remember that in the early days these glimpses may be fleeting. Within a short space of time they will become more substantial and clearer. Introduce yourself and ask the name of your guide. Don't expect a literal answer: the name, when it appears, will probably simply appear in your mind. When it does, don't forget to write it down!

Working with your Spirit Guides

Clarity when working with the spirit world and your own guides is important. Spirits can help and guide you in many ways; they also need some guidance as well! Contacting your spirit guides is about communication and this needs to be a two-way process. Be specific about your aims and goals or the help and assistance that you need from your guides. Never assume that a guide will know what you need from them.

When you feel ready to return to the physical world, begin the process slowly. Say your goodbyes and ask your guides to join you again in future sessions. Begin to sense your breathing again, clearly feeling the air enter and leave your body. It's likely that you will feel or see the "door" closing and at this point you can gradually open your eyes, focus on the room around you. If you use a candle, begin to focus clearly on the light it casts. Stretch and feel your physical body, sense and see the room around you, and slow your chanting to a stop.

Mundane Reality and Why it's Good for You

Once you are fully conscious again, make any notes you wish to record before opening the circle that you have cast (again, see the process described in Chapter 4). Generally, you will feel a little lightheaded after the process. This is perfectly normal and is a sensation that you will become accustomed to. Many practitioners recommend eating or drinking something warm at this stage; it's a good way to reconnect with the physical world and will help to bring you back "down to earth". In fact, any physical activity is good after contacting the spirit world; vacuuming or taking a run both work equally well. Both have all the right elements of real, daily, slightly boring practicality which will help you to reconnect with this world. Choose an activity that gets your body moving and reminds you of the mundane!

Chapter 7
The Ways of the Spirit World

Before we incarnate in the physical world, we set goals for ourselves: tasks and lessons that we must complete to aid in our evolution as spirits and in our journey towards enlightenment. Unfortunately, we all go through a period of amnesia as we are born into this world. Although those goals are real and do exist, few souls remember them in the chaos of incarnating in the physical world!

The role that our guides play is to help in our efforts to achieve these goals. We often chose our guides for specifically this purpose before we incarnate. Spirit guides are aware of our needs and their main function is to help us to work towards these goals. This help means that we often find exactly what we need, just when we need it most, in the most unlikely of circumstances and places.

This help and guidance take place all of the time, and once you are attuned to it, you'll be surprised at just how much help you can obtain – not to mention already have obtained in the past! Spirit guides are adept at putting the resources to achieve our goals in place, be those resources people, money, books or even locations.

It's important to understand that spirit guides help us to accomplish the purpose that we have set ourselves. Demands for our spirit guides to source large and plentiful amounts of money may not be met if this does not serve a purpose within our own spiritual goals and needs. Of course, if it does, then it may well come your way!

Clarity and Reality

As mentioned in the previous chapter, clarity is extremely important when working with spirit guides. But why? Surely, they know what you want, need, and what will benefit you most? The truth is that most spirit guides will not naturally act or interfere without our permission or without a very specific request. While spirit guides do arrange parts of our life to offer us the best opportunities to achieve what we need to, they don't like to interfere with our free will. Throughout our lives we are faced with a series of choices which all affect our future; spirit guides will ensure that options are there which will help us to further our goals but they generally don't insist that we take them. Nor do they get upset if we don't!

Being clear in what you need, and why, will actively get your spirit guides furnishing you with the means to achieve the desired results. For example, don't simply say to your guide, "I would like to pay my mortgage off". Thirty years later this may well happen, as it would anyway, and your request will have been met! Phrasing the request more specifically (and realistically) may go something like this; "I would like to pay X amount, extra, off my mortgage this year. Please help me to find the resources and the opportunities to achieve this".

While clarity is important, leave your spirit guides some room for maneuver. In the example above, don't simply demand more hours at work in order to achieve your goal; allow the guides and the universe to come up with a way to achieve it. It may not be quite what you expect, but it will come.

Praying for Miracles

When working with spirit guides, don't pray or beg. People who have a religious background often approach working with spirits in this manner. The spirits guides that you encounter are your equals; they may be able to see the world and opportunities around you more clearly, but they are there to help, not to donate gifts or bestow favors. Your guides will view you as eminently worthy of the help they can give, and they are very much on your side. Many approach spirits in a supplicant manner but remember that your guides are working for you. They are not "superior" in any sense, they're on your side!

Getting to Know You

Treat your guides just as you would friends in the physical world. Get to know their names as soon as possible! This information may be forthcoming from the start, but it may take a little while for you to be sure. Simply ask, it's only polite after all! While the guides that you encounter will be very much on your side, they may be shy, reticent at first, and need some coaxing to reveal information to you. Don't start asking for your needs to be met at first, simply start by getting to know each other. You wouldn't approach an acquaintance or friend in that manner, right? Be respectful with you guides and show them kindness.

Communication without Technology

Spirit guides communicate with us in a way which is most suited to both us and them. The most common ways are through clairvoyance, clairaudience, claircognizance and clairsentience. Clairvoyance is the most commonly recognized of these; in this case a very clear image will appear in your mind's eye. This is also the most common with people who are very visual in their lives. Clairaudience is similar but will take the form of words being spoken in your head; a little disturbing for those who have not experienced it before, but actually most people will have this experience at some point in their lives. The words may come in the form of a song that appears in your mind, for no apparent reason, and this is likely to be a message from your guide.

Claircognizance is simply the process where thoughts begin to appear in your head. The thoughts may seem random, to have come from nowhere and have the "quality" of a memory, although they'll most likely relate to experiences to come, or actions to take in the future. Again, being aware of this inner knowledge and where it is coming from is important, and you should take notice of any messages that appear in this way.

Clairsentience takes the forms of physical feelings. An itch here, or a pricking there. These subtle prompts can take time to recognize, interpret and understand. Once you've established the meanings of these coded messages, you'll be able to interpret what they mean and what action you should take.

Mysterious Moves

Spirit guides aren't above using earthly technology to communicate with us. Some may use television, radio, or even the computer. Seeing programs or news bulletins when the TV is off (although you may only realize it was off later) or finding yourself on a web page that you are certain you didn't navigate to are sure signs that a message is trying to get through to you. As they say, spirits do move in very mysterious ways, and some of those ways include the click of a mouse!

Chapter 8
Who Exactly Are You Dealing With?

Some entities are not what they seem, and for those new to working with spirit guides it's important to work out what you are dealing with. Many people will use a Ouija Board at some point in their dealings with the spirit world, and this and other methods of contacting spirits can lead to some unwelcome guests. We've already taken a look at how to rid ourselves of these unwanted presences, and in this chapter, we look at how to identify types of spirit that may not be what they seem.

The Good Guys

Our spirit guides have our best interests at heart. It's in their interests as much as ours to help us on our path through this life. That is their main motivation, and spirits that have chosen to be a spirit guide are making a conscious choice, to aid with their own evolution and spiritual development. They are usually the spirits of those who have lived here on earth in the past and who have achieved a higher state of consciousness. Before progressing further in their enlightenment, they have chosen to act as guides, for our benefit and as part of their own journey.

In theory this makes genuine spirit guides easy to identify. The following tips will also help!

- Guides will always be positive, helpful, and make you feel positive about yourself. They will accept that you are in charge of your life and that you must make choices, and their role is simply helping to put the right things and circumstances in your path.

- Guides do not instruct you as to what you should do. They are guides, just that, not leaders. They may come up with suggestions that they believe will benefit you, but they won't insist that you take these up.

- You will not find that a genuine guide will become angry, sulky or berate you. They are supportive, loving, and generous. While a guide won't flatter your ego, they will encourage you to believe in yourself and your own strength.

- Spirit guides will support you equally through the good and bad times in life. They will not let you wallow in self-pity or allow you to take on a victim mentality. With love and care they'll help to find a way through life's difficult times.

The Less Than Good Guys

Looking for a being which is gentle, beneficial, caring, and offering support will help you to identify your true guides. However, there are very clear signals that the "guide" you have found is not a genuine spirit guide and is more interested in its own agenda. The following traits will help to identify when a spirit guide is not all that it seems:

- The guide tells you that they have never contacted anybody in the past and have only contacted you because you are "special".

- The guide says that you have opened doorways, portals, or gates to other worlds and that nobody else has been able to do this in the past.

- The guide becomes grumpy and petulant when your friends express disbelief in its existence or are cynical about the messages it is giving you.

- Odd things begin to happen in your life and the spirit claims it's there to protect you. It suggests that an evil spirit is trying to harm you but, coincidentally, is itself always there when these occurrences happen!

- The spirit says that it needs your help, usually to write, speak, or take action in the world. It claims that only you can help it in this way.

- The spirit seems to be focused on how special you are, how intuitive you are and is fostering a sense of self-aggrandizement.

From the above examples, you should be able to see that spirits and entities that exist in the spirit world are not intrinsically that different from those of us living on a physical plane of existence. The different types are very familiar to most of us from people and friends that we already have in the physical world. Generous, caring and giving or needy, moody, and jealous; we've all met these types of "real" people and in your journey within the spirit world you'll almost certainly encounter different types of spirit. As you become more adept it will prove easy to "spot" the genuine kind of spirit guide over the less helpful type.

For those of you have unfortunately found yourselves with the latter, making a simple request to leave is nearly always the most you will need to do. Don't be fearful, or afraid of retribution; spirits will, in nearly all cases accept your request. Keep in mind that this request should be made firmly by use of straightforward language that makes it clear that there is no place for this spirit in your life and it should leave. See Chapter 5 for simple ways to achieve this.

However, if all else fails and you are continuing to find it difficult to rid yourself of an unwelcome spiritual guest, consider contacting a friend who is attuned to the spirit world to work together on breaking the link. Or a qualified psychic with experience of dealing with these less then helpful house-guests!

Chapter 9
Building Spiritual Relationships

In this last chapter we'll explore some practical tips and tricks to working with your spirit guides. I hope this book has already taught you the basic methods you can use to access and communicate with your spirit guides. This chapter is designed to reinforce the lessons you have learned and to introduce further practical steps to working with your spirit guides.

The relationship with your guides is going to be a lifelong one and, in most cases, your own spirit guides will have a very unique way of working with you. Over time you will become familiar with these quirks and the personalities of your guides. To start with, the information in this chapter should help you to negotiate your way through the early stages of working with your guides. Eventually that fine tuning will pay off, and communication will be clear and smooth, and messages will be obvious.

Believing Is Seeing

Belief is key to working with the spirit world. Even if you are skeptical at first, suspend that disbelief and be open to what you experience in your first meditations. While a little healthy skepticism is no bad thing in daily life, it will make it harder to connect with your spirits. At this stage in your journey, peacefully go with the flow and learn to recognize your spirit guides and accept their wisdom.

The Voices Told Me to Do It!

Hearing voices does not mean you're mad. If this worries you, you're not alone! It is a concern for a lot of people at first, but remember that "auditory hallucinations" have been experienced throughout history and, along with visions, these have often ended up forming the basis of major world religions and sacred texts– including a couple you might have heard of. Similarly, in classical times muses were an entity accepted as "real" and considered to guide artists and writers most constructively.

Brain Functions

Your left-side of the brain is the most likely source for doubt and worry about going a bit mad! It deals primarily with the conscious world and practical, everyday realities. It's likely that it will argue you are just talking to yourself or losing the plot. Switch it off! Let your intuition guide you in your meditations. You'll be pleasantly surprised at the experiences and knowledge you will gain. Besides, you're in control of this experience, and you choose when to switch it off and when to come back to the physical.

Switching off from Reality (in a Good Way)

Learn early on to switch off from the physical world. Meditation techniques can help, and creating a quiet, undisturbed, sacred space in which to commune with your spirit guides is essential.

Clear Intentions and Instructions

Make your intentions clear when you meet your spirit guides. You are looking for assistance and guidance in life and need solid help, in the real world, to help you achieve your goals. This relationship is part friendship, part guidance and part "working" relationship. Be sure that your guides understand this from the start, although they will be relatively clear on this.

Building Trust

Trust what your guides tell you once you have begun to establish your relationship with them. "Tell" in this sense often comes in the form of a specific vision or set of words. It can also take the form of "gut" feeling. Trust the first image, words, or feeling that comes into your mind when you are seeking guidance. The first answer is nearly always the most relevant.

Humor and Coincidence

Many spirit guides have a sense of humor. They won't poke fun at you, but they may deliver answers in a rather unique and sometimes laughable way. If the answer to your question is not forthcoming during a session, keep an eye out for it in your daily life. It could turn up on a billboard unexpectedly, over the radio when you're only half listening, or in an anecdote told to you by a complete stranger on a train or bus.

Tools to Aid Communication

Ouija boards and pendulums can be helpful for those who do not have strong clairvoyant or similar abilities. Ouija boards do have a "spooky" reputation, but this is simply because they are overused by those inexperienced in dealing with the spirit world. Thanks to this fact, it is true that they can be one way in which to become saddled with a troublesome or unwanted spirit. This can be avoided by easily using sensible precautions, such as casting a circle, asking for protection from your spirit guides, opening the circle and cleansing, or smudging once you have completed the séance.

A pendulum is also a useful tool, and it is simple to make one from a weight and some string. Define for yourself the swing which means "yes" and that which means "no". Most people find that this simple technique is extremely effective although for some it can be a little unsettling at first. Again, it cannot be emphasized enough, remember to use proper protective spells, rituals, or prayers at the start of each session.

Repetition, Repetition, Repetition

Always keep an eye out for repetition in your life, in particular repeated images, words, or symbols. These are invariably a sign that your spirit guide is trying to tell you something important – and with a sense of urgency. In most cases the image, word, or message will be crystal clear. If it's not, then conduct a session to contact your guide or guides at the first opportunity.

Synchronicity

Spirit guides are not above using synchronicity as a technique to get your attention and/or offer guidance. It is, in fact, one of their favorite tools. Synchronicity was first described by Carl Jung and describes the process whereby meaningful coincidences occur in life. A simple example would be when you are wondering whether or not to take a journey to a new place, and a vehicle drives past with a sticker promoting that place. Synchronicity often comes in small ways but, as with any advice from your spirit guides, it should be taken seriously.

Your Choice and Your Choices

One thing that should be emphasized when working with spirits is that you have free will. Luckily, your guides will not only recognize this but respect it. While some individuals can become obsessed with working with their spirit guides, this is rarely a good idea. When it comes to the big decisions in life (marrying, divorcing, moving home, or starting a new job) consider all the factors involved. The real, practical details of how the change or decision will affect your life and the long-term implications. The spirits will offer you advice and guidance, but the decision must always be yours. When you've come to your conclusion, your instinct of what is right and wrong for you will almost certainly confirm that you are making the right decision.

The Amazing World of Spirit

Working with your spirit guides to create the best opportunities in your life and finding the right path for yourself is an amazing, enlightening experience. For those who have worked in this way for many years, it becomes normal, and they find that the advice and opportunities they have found in the world of the spirit are invaluable. If you are beginning on your journey, just getting to know your guides and learning how to interpret their advice, the experience will be truly amazing. I hope that you find a great deal of success in your journey with your spirit guides and that this book has been able to help you take those first steps. Be patient with yourself, and most importantly, enjoy these new spirit world connections! You are of infinite worth and this adventure in enlightenment is sure to hold meaningful discoveries.

Conclusion

Thank you again for choosing this book!

I hope this book was able to help you to learn the basic, practical steps to working with your own spirit guides. The lessons and guidance you can find from the spirit world will be invaluable in helping to achieve your goals in this life (and beyond). I wish you the best of luck.

Finally, if you enjoyed this book, please take the time to share your thoughts and post a review on Amazon. It'd be greatly appreciated!

Thank you and good luck!

Your friend,

Mia Rose

Other books by Mia Rose

Astral Projection: The Beginners Guide on How to Travel Out of Your Body on the Astral Plane

Astrology: The Complete Guide to the Zodiac Signs

Auras: How to See Human Aura Colors In 7 Easy Steps

Chakras & Mudras for Beginners: Mudras for Balancing and Awakening Chakras

Chakras for Beginners: Understanding Chakras, Chakra Balancing and Chakra Healing

Creative Visualization: 6 Positive Days of Guided Visualization Techniques - Unlock Creative Thinking and your Life Potential Through Meditation

Crystals: The Ultimate List of Crystals and Their Uses

Dowsing: 30 Amazing Things You Can Do with Dowsing

Dreams: Dream Interpretation for Beginners - Uncover the Hidden Meanings of Your Dreams

Lucid Dreaming: Learn How to Control Your Dreams in 10 Easy Steps

Magical Chants: 30 Magical Chants, Spells and Rituals for Health, Wealth and Love

Meditation for Beginners: Learn How to Easily Relieve Stress, Achieve Mindfulness, and Live Peacefully in Your Everyday Life

Mindfulness for Beginners: Discover the Best Way to Preserve Your Peace of Mind

Numerology: The Ultimate Guide to Uncovering Your Future, Creating Success and Making Your Dreams a Reality Using the Art and Science of Numbers

Palmistry: Palm Reading for Beginners - The 72 Hour Crash Course on How to Read Your Palms and Start Fortune Telling Like a Pro

Reiki: Reiki for Beginners - Learn the Ancient Art of Reiki Healing and Transform Your Life!

Tarot Card Meanings: The 72 Hour Crash Course and Absolute Beginner's Guide

Third Eye: Third Eye Awakening for Beginners in 5 Easy Steps

Wealth Magic: 15 Steps to Attract Wealth, Create Prosperity and Manifest Money

Wicca for Beginners: Spells, Candles and Witchcraft for the Complete Beginner

Yoga for Beginners: 35 Yoga Poses for Women, Men, Kids and Seniors

Made in the USA
Coppell, TX
14 December 2021